An Aussie's Guide To ..

SPEAKING AUSTRALIAN

So ... ya wanna visit good ol Oz.
Well good onya mate, bout time you decided to drop in for a yarn.
Better sharpin up ya aussie lingo and get ya butt over here cause ya gonna have a ripper of a time.

by (Born n' Bred Aussie Lad) George Lee Sye

MAIN TOPICS

I got a story to tell ya -- Start speaking aussie

SOARENT PUBLISHING
PO Box 267, Ravenshoe, Qld, AUSTRALIA, 4888

georgeleesye.com/books

© All rights reserved by George Lee Sye (2011)

CONTENTS

I Got A Story To Tell Ya 4

Where'd It Come From? 6

Start Speaking Aussie 9

    A 9

    B 14

    C 31

    D 40

    E 46

    F 47

    G 52

    H 59

    I 62

    J 63

    K 65

    L 68

    M 71

    N 75

    O 77

P	80
Q	86
R	87
S	92
T	102
U	106
V	107
W	108
X	110
Y	110
Z	111
That's It Mate	112

SPEAKING AUSTRALIAN

I Got A Story To Tell Ya

Me dad had just got back from his trip to the states. And holy cow was he chatty about it .... skitin about the big flash places he stayed and the food he scoffed down. Even told me about the biggest pile a flamin pancakes he'd ever seen in life.

But most of all he was blown away by how the Americans got bamboozled when he spoke to em.

He was tryna get out of the airport and go to a hotel after he got to LA. He had never been there before in his life and was walkin around like some goose from the bush; checkin out the big tall buildings and ginormous size of the airport. Now he reckoned the best way to get outa the place was ta catch a taxi so he walked out to the road where they parked. As he walked up to one of those bright yellow taxis, this bloke who looked like he didn't have a brass razoo got out, he was obviously the driver. Me dad said "gidday mate, can I get a lift with you?" The bloke said he could so me dad said "Ya blood's worth bottlin." Me dad then said "Would ya mind if I put me bag in the boot mate?"

Well blow me down if the driver didn't stop in his tracks and just stare at him like he was some kinda moron from out back of Bourke. Dad spoke in his normal fast aussie way of talkin, and when he said that it musta sounded to the driver like a machine gun spittin out a single word - "wouldjamindifIputmebaginthebootmate?"

He looked at me dad in disbelief, "what did you say sir?"

It took a while for dad to realise this bloke had no idea what a bag or a boot was. He was used to hearing them called suitcases and trunks. Not only that, he spoke so fast the words were jammed together like one big sound. No wonder the bloke was gobsmacked.

Ever since I was an ankle biter I thought nuthin about the way we talked as aussies. It was just our normal way of tellin yarns and givin each other an ear bashin. We just let er rip and everbody knows zactly what each other is sayin.

Wanna know sumthin .... I reckon next time I go to the states with me swag I'm gonna ask the same thing as me dad and checkout the driver's reaction.

SPEAKING AUSTRALIAN

Where'd It Come From?

Aussie slang is part of our culture. Interestingly, slang isn't limited to Aussie speak. In fact, slang is defined as:

> *(n) a type of language consisting of words and phrases that are regarded as very informal, are more common in speech than writing, and are typically restricted to a particular context or group of people*

Slang exists in every country and it is really a reflection of that country's culture and history. The way in which people play with words, assemble words and pronounce words tells us a lot about them.

The History Of Australian Slang

Aussie English shares a close relationship with English as spoken by people in Britain, but yes there are some differences. Obviously this relationship emerged from the way in which this country developed on the back of the penal colonies of the late 1700s and 1800s.

Much of the way we speak is a reflection of the history of this country.

We use words derived from Aboriginal language such a 'woomera, 'didgeridoo' and 'boomerang'. We talk about the 'outback' and 'cattle drives'. We also reflect on 'gold rushes' and 'bush rangers', using terminology that say a lot about the history of Australia.

What's really interesting now is that Aussie slang has been influencing the English language for decades. In fact many Australian English words now appear in the Oxford English Dictionary. online.

Here are some words that originated in Australia.

> *Digger means Australian soldier*

> *Yobo refers to An obnoxious and a loud person with no social and behavioural skills*

Outback means Sparsley populated, remote area

Fair go means A fair deal

We also have words in our lingo that sound like they're Aussie, but in fact have Irish and British origins.

Here in Australia we use the word 'Sheila' as slang for woman. For example an Aussie might say - 'You found yourself a good sheila there mate!' Well Sheila is in fact a common girls name in Ireland (alternatively spelled Shelagh and Sheelagh) derived from the Irish name Síle, meaning 'heavenly'.

What about the good old Aussie word Billy? We call the enamel or tin cooking pot wth the wire handle we use to boil water on the camp fire a 'Billy'. That word has Scottish origins where billy -pot means 'cooking utensil'.

Truth is, Australian vocabulary is actually an amalgamation of many vocabularies including British English, Gaelic, Polynesian languages and the fantastic languages of Indigenous Australians.

We Shorten Words and Give Longer Words Nicknames

One thing you'll notice about Aussie slang is that the words are often references, or nick-names I guess, for longer words.

We must be a lazy bunch here in Australia ay? After shortening the long words we end up using then as day-to-day language. Here's a few examples:

Afternoon becomes 'arvo'

Journalist becomes 'journo'

Postman becomes 'postie'

Biscuit becomes 'bikkie'

Mosquito becomes 'mozzie'

Sunglasses becomes 'sunnies'

We also do the same to names of people even though the nickname sometimes becomes a longer word:

John or Johnathon is 'Johno'

David is 'Davo'

Michael becomes 'Mikey' or 'Mick'

Regardless of the guy's name, if he has red hair he might be called 'Blue'

Louis becomes 'Lou'

Yep, good ole Aussie lingo is fun, it's cool (in my opinion), becoming more widely known around the world, but most importantly remains deeply rooted in Australian history.

Just like the sound of the Didgeridoo is iconically Australian, so is our Aussie slang.

Start Speaking Aussie

Everything you need to know about Aussie slang and good ole Aussie lingo is laid out in the following pages in alphabetical order.

Enjoy.

A

Ace

Means something is excellent or very good

> *That's ace mate!*

AC/DC

Means bisexual

Aerial Ping Pong

Reference to Australian Rules football

Aggro

Means to be aggressive

> *If you do that your dad's gonna be aggro.*

All Ears

Means a person is listening

> *Tell me about it mage, I'm all ears.*

All The Go

Means its the trend, very popular

> *Painting pictures on latte is all the go now.*

Amber Fluid

Means beer

> *The amber fluid's gonna be flowin tonight.*

Anchors

Reference to the brakes on a car

> *When he pulled out in front of me I hit the anchors and just missed him.*

Ankle Biter

Reference to a small child, someone who bites your ankles

> *Hey Mick, you got any ankle biters yet?*

> *We just flew in on a plane fulla ankle biters.*

> *Holy crap, there's more ankle biters here than you can poke a stick at.*

Ant's Pants (or Bees Knees)

Means something is great, really good, the best

> *A sun roof in the tropics is the ants pants.*

Any Tic of the Clock

Means any moment, very soon, before you know it

> *He'll call any tic of the clock now.*

Ark Up

Means get angry or upset

> *He pulled me on about it in front of some customers so I arked up.*

Arse About

Means back the front, wrong way

> *He did the job all arse about.*

Arse Over Tit

Means to fall hard, severely

> *He fell arse over tit coming down the stairs.*

Arsey

Means to be very lucky

> *He's one arsey bugger.*
>
> *He has more arse than class.*

Arvo

Means the afternoon

> *Cya later this arvo.*
>
> *The game's on in the arvo just before the mozzies come out.*

Aussie

An Australian person

> *Checkout the aussies over by the bar.*

Aussie Salute

Brushing away flies with the hand

Av-a-go Ya Mug

Someone is not trying hard enough and you want them to, can also mean you want them to fight you

> *Come on, you're a big tough guy, have a go ya mug.*

Avo

Reference to an avocado

> *How bout some eggs and avo on toast for brekkie.*

Away With The Pixies

Mean to be dreaming

> *I was talking to me dad but wasn't any use cause he was away with the pixies.*

Ay

A commonly used expression (mostly in Queensland) which means do you agree

> *Looks like a good day ... ay.*

SPEAKING AUSTRALIAN

B

Back Hander

Refers to a bribe

> *Of course he got the job, he gave the guy a back hander to get it.*

Back of Bourke

Means a long way away

> *That bloke lives somewhere out back of bourke.*

Bad News

Means trouble

> *That bloke's bad news.*

Baffle With Bullshit

Means to trick or deceive someone with untruths and lies

Bag of Fruit

Reference to a man's suit

> *Checkout the bag of fruit that guy's wearin.*

Bail Out

To depart or leave something suddenly, often angrily

> *Hey mate, don't bail out now.*

Bail Somebody Up

Means to corner somebody in a physical way

> *I was walking past old mate's office and he bailed me up ... bloody hell.*

Balls And All

Means to be totally committed

> *No back out now, it's balls and all from here on.*

Balls Up

Means to make a big mistake

> *What a balls up that was, they were never going to get that approved.*

Banana Bender

Reference to someone from Queensland

Bang On (also Spot On)

Means exactly right

> *You're bang on with that statement.*

Barbie

Reference to a barbecue (noun)

> *Lets chuck a few sausages on the barbie.*

Barney

Reference to an argument

> *We got into a huge barney with those guys.*

Barrack

Means to cheer on or support a team or person in some form of competition

> *Who do you barrack for mate, the aussies or the kiwis?*

Bastard

Reference to an unpleasant or not so nice person

> *That's guys a real bastard in the way he treats his people.*

Can also be used as a form of affection for somebody you know well

> *What've you been doing you old bastard?*

Bathers

Swimming costume

> *I usually go swimming in my bathers.*

Battler

Means a hard worker only just making enough to support himself or his family

> *My dad was a real battler.*

Beat Around the Bush

Means to avoid getting to the point quickly

> *Can you stop beating around the bush and tell me what you want?*

Beak

Reference to a person's nose

> *He copped one right on the beak.*

Beaut / Bewdy / Beauty

Means great or fantastic, excited approval, something has gone really well

> *Bewdy mate, thanks for the help.*
>
> *What a beaut way to drive to work.*
>
> *Why you little bewdy, now we can do some serious fishing.*

Bee's Dick

Means a small amount, very small

> *He missed by a bee's dick.*

Bee's Knees

Means excellent, great, awesome

> *Those things you bought are the bees knees.*

Bell

Means to call

> *Can you give me a bell a bit later.*

Belt Up

An angry way of asking somebody to stop talking and be quite

> *You kids better belt up or I'm gonna come down there.*

Big Bikkies

Means expensive

> *Man ... I can't afford one of those new SS Utes, they cost big bikkies, especially the souped up version.*

Big Note

To brag or boast

> *This bloke's just big noting himself.*

Bikkie (pronounced bick.ie)

Reference to a biscuit

> *Chuck us a bikkie will you mum?*

Billabong

An old term that is reference to an ox-bow river or watering hole; not used much now but it's still part of history

> *Did you hear the song about the swagman camped by the billabong?*

Billie

This is a large tin can to boil water over a campfire

> *You start the fire and I'll chuck the billie on.*

Billy Cart

Reference to a child's toy cart, usually steered with rope tied to either end of the front axle

Bingle

Means a minor car accident

> *Had a bit of a bingle on the way to work this morning.*

Birthday Suit

Means to be naked

> *Walking around in his birthday suit.*

Bite

Means to ask for money

> *He put the bite on me for 50 bucks.*

Bitumen

Reference to the tar covering on a surfaced road

> *Road to Surfers is bitumen all the way.*

Black Stump

Means a long way away

> *He lives out past the black stump.*

Did His Block

Means to get angry

Bloke

A man or guy

> *Who's this bloke think he is?*

Blokey

Means to behave in a manly way or to be very manly

> *That's kind of a blokey thing to do.*

Blood's Worth Bottlin

Means a person is excellent, somebody who has been helpful

> *Thanks mate, your blood's worth bottlin.*

Bloody

Mean very, it magnifies something

> *This house is bloody huge mate.*

Bloody Oath

Means something is the truth

> *Bloody oath she did, we all saw her do it.*

Blow In

Reference to a stranger

> *Who's this blow in, never seen him before?*

Blow in the Bag

To undertake a breathalyzer test which tests for blood alcohol level

> *Cops pulled me over this arvo, had to blow in the bag.*

Blow Me Down

Means you were surprised or amazed

> *Well blow me down, she actually did it.*

Blow Your Dough

Means to spend all of your money

Blowing Through

Means to be in a hurry, not staying

> *I'm just blowing through mate.*

Bludger

Refers to a layabout or lazy bugger

> *Hey ya bludger, get off ya butt and help out.*

Blue

Means to fight or argue, also means to make a mistake

> *I got into a blue at the pub tonight, should've kept my mouth shut.*

> *Made a major blue this morning ... called the wife 'the old lady' to her face.*

Blue Murder

Means serious trouble

> *He cried blue murder.*

Blunder

Means a mistake

> *Made a blunder when I bought that old truck.*

Bob's Yer Uncle

Means if you do this (whatever is said first) it will work or be OK

> *Mate, just jump in ... give it a go and bob's yer uncle.*

Bodgy

Means a poor quality job

> *I got a plumber in yesterday and the bastard did a bodgy job. I gotta good mind to rip it into his boss.*

Bog In

Means to tuck in, commence eating

> *Two, four, six eight, bog in don't wait.*

Bogan

Reference to a young, immature person from a lower class area.

> *They're just a bunch of bogans.*

Boiler

Reference to an old woman

> *Check out the old boiler, she's been around for years.*

Bondi Cigar

Reference to feces floating in the sea

> *Was swimming near the river and got hit in the dial by a bondi cigar ... bloody hell ... I nearly spewed.*

Bonzer

Means great, awesome, very good

> *He's a bonzer guy that one, I love doing business with him.*
>
> *That's bonzer mate, never seen anybody do it that good before.*

Boofhead

Reference to a stupid or silly person

> *You're a boofhead mate.*

Bomb

Reference to an old run down motor car

> *I still drive that old bomb I bought back in the 80s.*

Boogie Board

Reference to a body board

> *Forget the surfin, try out the boogie board in this water.*

Boomerang

A wooden carved Aboriginal tool shaped like a V and used for hunting

> *These buggers went hunting with boomerangs, can you believe it.*

> *I bought one of those boomerangs the other day, gonna give it a go and see if it comes back.*

Booze

Means alcohol

Booze Bus

Reference to the police van used for breath testing drivers on the side of the road

> *Oh shit, there's the booze bus!*

Boozer

Reference to a pub

> *Oi, do ya wanna go down to the boozer for a few pots?*

Bored Shitless

Means really bored

Bottle Shop

Place where you go to buy alcohol

> *Might pop down to the bottle shop and grab a six pack.*

Bottler

Means something is excellent

> *What a bottler! Best damn bull I've ever seen.*

Bouncer

Somebody who provides door security at pubs and night clubs

> *Damn bouncers chucked me out last night, I musta had one too many pots.*

Brass

Means money

Brass Razoo

Reference to money, without it a person is poor

> *The guy is broke, he hasn't got a brass razoo left from his inheritance.*

Bread Basket

Reference to the stomach

> *He punched me right in the bread basket.*

Brekkie

Reference to breakfast

> *Meet ya downstairs for brekkie at 7 in the morning.*

Brickie

Reference to a bricklayer

> *Me mate spent his first few years workin as a brickie.*

Bring a Plate

Instruction to bring a plate of food to a party

> *Hey, don't come empty handed, everybody's gotta bring a plate.*

Brissie (or Brizzie)

Reference to Brisbane, the state capital of Queensland

> *Been livin in Brissie for a few years now ... love the place.*

Brown Eyed Mullet

Reference to feces floating in the sea

> *Checkout the brown eyed mullet ... I aint swimming there that's for sure.*

Buck's Night

Refer to stag party or stag night

Buckley's (or Buckley's Chance)

There's no chance

> *You've got buckley's of kicking that goal mate, it's too far away.*

Budgies (or Budgie Smugglers)

Reference to men's speedo style swimming costume as worn by professional swimmers and some politicians (lol)

> *You wearin boardies or budgies to the beach mate?*

Bugger

Reference to any person, mischievous person, exclamation

> *Check that bugger out.*
>
> *He's a little bugger.*
>
> *Aaaagh bugger it ... I'll go somewhere else.*

Buggered

Means to be very tired, exhausted

Buggered If I Know

Means you do not know

Brick Shithouse

Means to be solid, heavy, strong

> *He's built like a brick shithouse, must do weights or something.*

Bull Bar

A stout bar fixed to the front of a vehicle to protect it in case it hits something like a cow or kangaroo

> *Got a bull bar on the beast today mate, it's a ripper.*

Bull Dust

Reference to outback dust, could also mean something said is untrue or rubbish

> *That's bull dust mate, nobody could ever do that.*

Bullshit

Means something is rubbish

> *He came in telling everyone his bullshit.*

Bum Fluff

Refers to light hair on the face of an adolescent who cannot yet grow a proper beard

Bummer

An exclamation related to something that went wrong

> *What a bummer.*

Bunch of Fives

Means fist

> *You keep that up you'll get a bunch of fives right on the nose mate.*

Bundy

It's short for Bundaberg (town in Queensland), and it's also the brand of rum that's made there

> *I'll have a bundy and coke mate.*

Bush

Reference to the outback

> *I love camping in the bush.*

Bush Bashing

Means to go driving out in the bush somewhere, off the sealed road

Bush Telegraph

Reference to gossip, informal network that passes on information

Bush Telly

Reference to a campfire

> *Yeah mate, we just sat around the bush telly and told a few yarns.*

Bush Tucker

Reference to native outback food

> *Got a bit stuck so we had to live off bush tucker for a few days.*

Bush Week

Reference to some sort of slow work

> *So what do you think this is .... bush week?*

Bushie

Reference to someone who lives in the Bush

> *Old mate's a real bushie, never comes to the big smoke.*

Bushranger

Means outlaw

Ned Kelly is the most infamous of all the bushrangers.

BYO

A BYO restaurant is unlicensed and you have to Bring Your Own grog, BYO is the acronym for that

Let's checkout that Thai place near the mall, it's byo.

C

Cack

Means to laugh

> *I cacked myself when he said that.*

Cactus

Means dead or broken

> *Car's cactus mate ... you won't get that going again.*

Cadbury

Means a cheap drunk (a glass and a half)

> *That bloke's a real cadbury ... half an hour and he's under the table.*

Cake Hole

Reference to a person's mouth

> *Time to shut ya cake hole mate.*

Call It A Day

Means to end something

> *It's time to call it a day ladies.*

Can

Reference to the toilet

Back in a sec, gotta go to the can.

Cane It

Means to flog it, push it hard, drive very fast

> *He was caning it when he went past me, no wonder the cops were chasing him.*

Captain Cook

Means to look

> *Never been there ay ... let's have a captain cook then.*

Cark It

Means to die, used when something stops working

> *The engine's carked it mate, need a new one.*

Cheese and Kisses

Reference to the wife or missus

> *Well, time to get back to the cheese and kisses.*

Cheesed Off

Means to be angry or upset or annoyed

> *He was really cheesed off when I didn't turn up on time.*

Chewie

Reference to chewing gum

Wanna chewie mate?

Chocka

Means to be full, full up, filled

> *I'm chocka mate, couldn't fit another thing in.*

Choke a Darkie

Means to go to the toilet for number 2s

> *Well I'm off to choke a darkie.*

Chokkie (pronounced chock.ie)

Reference to chocolate

> *Man I feel like a chokkie, must be pregnant or something.*

Chop and Change

Means to keep changing continually

> *Ya can't pin him down, he keeps chopping and changing.*

Christmas Grip

Means someone has hold of a person's testicles

Chuck

Means to spew or vomit

> *Ooooo ... feel like I'm gonna chuck.*

Chuck a Yewy

Means to do a u turn

> *Shit ... that's the turn off back there ... chuck a yewy at the intersection up here.*

Chuffed

Means to be pleased, very happy with something

> *He was chuffed when he got that deal through.*

Chunder

Means to vomit

> *Oh man, I'm crook, gonna chunder if we don't get off this boat.*

Clanger

Reference to something that is a complete surprise, unanticipated

> *It was all going well then he dropped a clanger.*

Clapped Out

Means its no good anymore, won't work properly

> *The old truck's clapped out, I need a new one.*

Clayton's

Reference to a fake or substitute

> *That's a clayton's Rolex he got from Thailand.*

Clear as Mud

Means something does not make sense

> *Mate I hear ya, but that's clear as mud.*

Click

Reference to a kilometre -

> *How far? It's only about ten clicks away if I remember rightly.*

Clobber

Reference to clothes

> *Hey ... nice clobber mate, the chicks'll be flockin around you tonight.*

Clucky

Means to feel maternal

> *Now don't go getting all clucky now, I aint having anymore kids.*

Coat Hanger

Reference to a stiff arm across the neck.

> *When he hit him with that coat hanger it knocked him flat.*

Cobber

Means a friend

> *He's my cobber, we spent a lot of years together in the trenches.*

Cock Up

Reference to somethings that's gone wrong

> *What a cock up that was.*

Cocky

Reference to a farmer

> *Checkout the cocky over there, he's been working the land for years.*

It is also reference to a cockatoo

> *Pulled up in the paddock this arvo and there were cockies everywhere, bloody noisy things they are.*

Coffin Nail

Refers to a cigarette

Coldie

Reference to a beer

> *Chuck us a coldie will you Jack?*

Come a Gutser

Means to make a bad mistake or have an accident

> *He tried real hard but came a gutser, hope he's gonna be alright.*

Came Good (or Come Good)

Means to turn out ok

> *Market was dead for years but eventually it came good.*

Chook With Its Head Cut off

Means running about without any direction, erratic

> *He's been running around like a chook with its head cut off.*

Common as Dog Shit

Means very common

Compo

Reference to Workers' Compensation pay

> *Old mate is on compo these days, something about a crook back I hear.*

Not Within Cooee (or Get Within Cooee)

Figuratively this means a long way away

> *He tried to hit the target but couldn't get within cooee of it.*

Cook

Reference to the wife

> *Goin home to the cook guys, had enough for one night.*

Cooking With Gas

Means doing very well

> *After a few lessons he was cooking with gas.*

Corroboree

Means an aboriginal dance festival

> *Did you see Crocodile Dundee, I mean the bit where they had that corroboree out in the bush and the sheila was trying to take their photos?*

Counter Lunch

Reference to a pub lunch

> *Might grab a counter lunch today, sick of eating pies.*

Cozzie

Reference to a swimming costume

> *Let's chuck on the cozzies and get some sun and surf, what do ya reckon?*

Crack a Fat

Means to get an erection

Crack a Tinnie

Means to open a can of cold beer

> *Thats a fair day's work boys, time to crack a tinnie and chill out.*

Crack Onto

Means to try and chat up or make a pass at someone

> *I'm gonna see if I can crack onto that chick.*

Crash Hot

Means really good

> *The party was crash hot.*

Cranky

Means somebody is in a bad mood or angry

> *Man, stay away from Jim, he's one cranky old fart.*

Cream Em

Means to beat or defeat by a large margin

> *Beat em! Are you kidding .. we're gonna cream em.*

Crook

Means to be sick, not good

> *He was crook so I sent him home.*

Is also reference to a dishonest person or even criminal

> *The guy's a crook, don't listen to him.*

Cunning as a Dunny Rat

Means very cunning

Curly

A nickname for somebody who is bald

Cut Lunch

Means sandwiches

D

Dag

Reference to a funny person, nerd

> *What a dag that guy is,*

Daks (or Dacks)

Means trousers

Damage

Refers to the cost of something

> *What's the damage mate?*

Damper

The name for bread made from flour and water and usually cooked in foil on a camp fire

Date

Reference to a person's bum or behind

> *In the old days, the cops used to kick us up the date and send us on our way.*

Dead Horse

Means sauce

> *Pass the dead horse will ya mate.*

Dead Set

Means true or the truth

> *Dead set? Is that for real?*
>
> *Dead set mate, it really happened.*

Dero

Reference to a tramp, hobo, homeless person (originates from derelict)

Dial

Means your face

> *What's that smug look on your dial for?*

Didgeridoo

This is a uniquely Aboriginal musical instrument made from hollowed out branches or tree trunks

Digger

Reference to an Australian soldier

Dill

Means idiot

> *Check this dill out, he'll kill himself if he jumps off that.*

Dilly Bag

Name for an Aboriginal carrying bag

Ding

Means to dint something

> *I dinged the car mum, sorry.*

Ding Bat

Referring to somebody as a tool

> *Fancy doin that, he's a ding bat.*

Dingo's Breakfast

Means to go without breakfast

Dinki Di

Means the real thing, something is genuine

> *This is a dinki di scarab from an egyptian tomb.*

Dipstick

Means fool or idiot

> *Who does this dipstick think he is?*

Do Ya Block (Do My Block)

Means to get angry

> *No need to do ya block mate, it's just an accident.*

Dob In

Means to inform or tell on somebody

If you saw it you better dob him in to the cops before he does it again.

Docket

Means a receipt like you get out of a point of sale cash register when you buy something

Docoi

Reference to a documentary

Dog and Bone

Means telephone

> *I'll jump the dog and bone and call you.*

Dog's Breakfast

Means a big mess

> *That meeting was a dog's breakfast.*

Dole Bludger

Somebody who doesn't work and chooses to live on government handouts referred to as the dole

Donger (also Doodle and Dick)

Reference to a man's penis

Donk

Refers to the engine of a car

> *What size donk you got under the bonnet?*

Donkey's Years

Means a very long time

> *I haven't seen him in donkey's years.*

Doozy

Means something significant, extreme, outstanding

> *Man what a night ... that was a doozy.*

Doughnut (and Doughies)

Refers to driving a car in a circle and smoking the wheels

Down the Gurgler

Means something didn't pan out that well, it failed, its gone

Down Under

Reference to Australia

Drink With The Flies

Means to drink alone

Driving the Porcelain Bus

Means to spew or vomit in the toilet

Drongo

Reference to a dopey or stupid person

> *What a bunch of drongos, they should know better than to do burnouts in the city.*

Drop Kick

Reference to someone who is useless

> *That guy is a drop kick.*

Drop Your Guts

Means to fart or pass wind

> *Hey mate, did you drop your guts just then?*

Dry as a Dead Dingo's Donger

Very dry ... obviously

Dunny

Reference to the outside toilet, also called an outhouse

Dunny Paper

Means toilet paper

Durry

Means a cigarette

Dutch Oven

Refers to being under the covers when somebody farts

E

Ear Bashing

Means to be nagged

> *Man she gave me an ear bashing when I got home. Aint going out that late again.*

> *The oldies gave me one helluva ear bashing when I pranged their car.*

Eat a Horse

Means very hungry

> *Man, I could eat a horse.*

Elbow Grease

Means to put effort into a bit of work

> *You gotta put some elbow grease into it if you want to get it clean.*

Esky

A coolbox, something you put ice in before you fill it with drinks or food

Even Stevens

Means we are square, nobody owes anything to anyone

> *We're even stevens mate.*

Every Man And His Dog

Reference to the broader general public

> *Every man and his dog was there.*

Exy

Means expensive

> *Wow ... that's a bit exy. Not sure I can afford that.*

F

Fag

Means cigarette

> *Time for a fag mate.*

Fair Crack of the Whip (also Fair Suck of the Sav)

Means give me a fair go

> *Fair crack of the whip mate, you drove here, it's my turn to drive.*

Fair Dinkum

Means true, real, genuine

> *That's a fair dinkum Albert Namagira painting ya know, gonna be worth a quid in a few years time.*

> *This guy's fair dinkum ... we should give him a chance.*

Far Enough

Refers to agreement

> *Fair enough, let's do it then.*

Fair Go

Means you want a chance or a break

> *Come on mate, fair go ... how about I drive halfway then.*

Fang It

Means to drive very fast

> *If you want to get there on time you'll have to fang it.*

Fanny

Reference to a woman's vagina

Fart Arsing

Means to muck around and waste time

> *Better stop fart arsing about if you want to keep your job.*

Fella (or Fellow)

Reference to a man

> *He's not a bad fella.*

Fifty Ks South of Whoop Whoop

Means out in the middle of nowhere, a long way from here

Figjam

A person referred to as a figjam is someone who has a high opinion of themselves

Fire Away

Means to start speaking

> *Okay, fire away mate.*

Fish Out Of Water

Means to not fit in

> *He was like a fish out of water at his wife's tupperware party.*

Fisho

A fisherman

Fit as a Mallee Bull

Mean very fit and strong

> *Age has nothing to do with it, that guy's as fit as a mallee bull.*

Five Finger Discount

Means to it was obtained by stealing

Five O'clock Shadow

Means to be unshaven, its that light stubble that appears at the end of the day

Flake

Name given to shark fillets

Flake Out

Means to collapse or go to sleep

> *The guy flaked out while I was talking.*

Flap Your Gums

Means to talk a lot

> *Stop flappin your gums mate, we all need a turn here.*

Flat Chat (also Flat Out or Flat Out Like a Lizard Drinking)

Means going very fast at what ever they're doing

> *He's working flat chat mate, any faster and he'll bust a foo foo valve.*

Give it the Flick

To get rid of something

Flicks

Refers to the movies

> *So are you going to the flicks tonight?*

Flog

Means to sell and can also mean to steal

I'm gonna flog the old truck and get myself a new one.

That little shit flogged the truck while it was out the front of my place.

Fly The Coop

Means to leave

He's on his own now, she flew the coop last week.

Fly Wire

Reference to the screen covering over a window or doorway designed to keep insects out of the house

Footy

Reference to football - it does include Australian Rules (Victoria, South Australia and Western Australia mainly), Rugby League (New South Wales and Queensland), Rugby Union and Soccer

Franger

Reference to a condom

Sat on the bench and there was a franger on it ... bloody disgusting.

He opened his wallet and a franger fell out ... we pissed ourselves laughing.

Freckle

Reference to bum or anus

Couldn't see anything but his freckle disappearing into the distance.

Fruit Loop

Reference to somebody who is a fool

Full as a Goog (also Full as a Boot)

Means to have drunken or eaten to the excess

Fulla Shit

Means they tell lies, make stuff up

> *Don't listen to him, he's fulla shit.*

Full On

Means someone is very intense

> *That bloke is just full on all the time, he never lets up.*

Furphy

Means a rumour, something that's not true

> *They reckon the moon landing took place in a shed and was staged but I think that's just a furphy.*

G

Gab

Means talk

Galah

Reference to a stupid person

That bloke's a galah, glad he didn't come to my party.

Gander (also Gawk)

Means look at something

> *Take a gander at this mate.*

Gas Bag

Means a person never shuts up, always talking

> *What a gas bag, my ear is still ringing from the ear bashing he gave me.*

Gidday

Means hello

Gift of the Gab

Means a person can really talk

> *That guy's got the gift of the gab alright, he never stopped talking.*

Galah

Means fool, also loud, rudely behaved person

Game

Means up for it

> *I'm game, are you?*

Garbo

Somebody who collects the garbage from the front of houses

Get on the Turps

Means to drink alcohol

Get Rooted (also Get Stuffed)

A form of abuse, means no

> *You want me to do what? You can go and get rooted.*

Get The Shits

Means to get angry

> *Man has he got the shits tonight.*

Get Up Somebody

Means to rebuke a person, to rip it into them, tell them off

Give a Shit

Means to care

> *She doesn't give a shit.*

Give Birth to a Politician

Means to defecate

Give Lip

Means to give cheek to someone

> *Don't you give me lip mate or I'll plant a knuckle sandwich on ya.*

Give It a Burl

Means to try it, to have a go

Give It Away

Means to give up

> *Time to give it away buddy, this will never work.*

Give the Flick

Means to dump your partner (girlfriend or boyfriend)

Give You The Drum

Means to tip-off

> *Let me give you the drum ... back number 5 in the Melbourne cup ... guaranteed winner.*

Go Ape Shit

Means to get very angry

> *He found out about it and went ape shit.*

Gob Full

Means to abuse verbally

> *I didn't do my homework and man did she give me a gob full.*

Go Like the Clappers (also Go Like A Shower of Shit)

Means to go very fast, very powerful

His car goes like the clappers.

Going Off

Means a place is really humming with fun and frivolity

We went next door to that new club and it was really going off.

Going to the Dunny

Means off to the toilet

Gone Walkabout

Means a person has wandered off, is lost, can't be found

I tried to find my mate but he'd gone walkabout.

Goner

Means finished, forget about it

Jim's a goner if he keeps doing that.

Gone to the Pack

Means to have gotten worse, gone bad

Jim's gone to the pack.

Gonna (also Gunna)

Means going to

He's gonna do it later.

Good On Ya

Means well done

Goss

Means gossip, latest news

What's the goss mate?

Go To Buggery

Means no, get lost

They can go to buggery, I'm not paying carbon tax.

Grab By the Balls

Means to impress somebody

His presentation really grabbed me by the balls.

Green Around the Gills

Means to be sea sick or air sick

He's looking a bit green around the gills.

Greenie

A person who is an environmentalist, somebody concerned about and often protests in relation to environmental issues

Grinnin Like a Shot Fox

Reference to somebody who is very happy, smugly satisfied

> *They won the game and he sat there grinnin like a shot fox for the rest of the night.*

Grizzle

Means to complain or whinge

> *What's he grizzling about?*

Grog

Means alcohol

Grot

Reference to somebody who is untidy or dirty

> *The kids just don't clean up, they're a pair of grots.*

Grouse

Means great, terrific

Gut Full of Piss

Means to be full of alcohol, drunk

Gutser

Means to fall

> *He tried to jump three stairs at once and came a gutser.*

H

Hack

Means to cope with

He left cause he couldn't hack it.

Had It

Means thats the end, no more, to run out of patience with something

I've had it mate, I'm not taking it any more.

Half Your Luck

Means you are very lucky

Half your luck mate, wish I could get the same result as you.

Hammie

Means hamstring

He pulled a hammie.

Hang on a Tic

Means wait a minute, stop what you're doing

Hey, hang on a tic, what do you mean by that?

Happy as a Pig in Shit (also a Pig in Mud)

Means very happy

Have a Bo Peep

Means to take a look

Have a Burl (also Give it a Burl)

Means to try or attempt something

> *Just have a burl, see out it turns out.*

Have a Lend Of

Means to take advantage of someone or to tease

> *Don't worry about that guy, he's just havin a lend of you.*

Have a Naughty

Means to have sex

Heaps

Means a lot

> *Got heaps of em mate.*

Hit the Toe

Means to run

> *Before I could grab him he hit the toe and was gone.*

Hit the Frog and Toad

Means road

> *Well that's it for me, time to hit the frog and toad.*

Hit the Piss

Means to drink alcohol

Hit the Nail on the Head

Means exactly right, correct

Hit the Sack

Means to go to bed

> *Time to hit the sack, cya.*

Holy Dooly (or Holy Crap)

Simply an expression of surprise

> *Holy dooly ... you own that thing!*

Hoon

Reference to a hooligan

> *These guys are just hoons.*

Hooroo

Means goodbye

Hottie

Means a really good looking person, usually a girl or woman

> *Man she is a hottie.*

Howzit Goin

A greeting, same as gidday

Hurl

Means to vomit

Idiot Box

Means television

Iffy

Means dodgy

>*Not sure I'd buy it, looks a bit iffy to me.*

In a Tic

Means in a moment

>*Yeah I'll do it in a tic.*

In the Good Books

Means you've done something good and its been recognised by somebody else

>*I bought her flowers this morning, now I'm in the good books.*

In the Know

Means you have confidential or inside information

I'm in the know mate.

In the Shit

Means you're in trouble

Man ... I'm in the shit now.

It's a Goer

Means something will definitely occur

That deal is a goer mate, they loved your presentation.

J

Jackaroo

Reference to a male person who works on a station and does tasks like mustering

Jillaroo

Reference to a female who works on a station and does tasks like mustering

Jack Of

Means fed up with

I'm jack of it now, time to move on.

Jack Shit

Means nothing

He knows jack shit about it.

At the end of the day, I finished with jack shit.

Jaffle

Reference to a toasted sandwich, usually made in a jaffle iron on an open fire

Jiffy

Means short time period

> *I'll be there in a jiffy.*

Job Somebody

Means to hit or punch somebody

Jocks

Reference to male underpants of the bikini style, not boxers

Joe Blogs (also Joe Blow)

Reference to any ole person

> *Looks like Joe Blogs over there wants to be first in the door when it opens.*

Journo

Means journalist

Jumped Up

Means stuck up or snobby

> *I don't know what's wrong with him, he's all jumped up.*

K

Kangaroo Loose in the Top Paddock

Means somebody is intellectually inadequate, not that smart, bit crazy

> *Watch that guy, something not quite right about him ... I think he's got a kangaroo loose in the top paddock.*

Kafuffle

Reference to some commotion

> *What's all the kafuffle here?*

Kaput

Means broken, stuffed, no good

> *The air conditioner's kaput now, no point turning it on.*

Keen as Mustard

Means very keen to do something

Keg on Legs

Reference to a big guy who is shaped like a keg, drinks a lot of beer

Kero

Means kerosene

Kick In (also Chip In)

Means to give or donate, to contribute some money

> *Hey guys, its time to kick in a few bucks each to pay for the pizza.*

Kick the Bucket

Means to die

Kindie

Means kindergarten and child care centre

Kiwi

Means somebody from New Zealand

Knackers

Reference to a male person's testicles

> *Yeah mate, got kicked right in the knackers ... dropped me like a ton of bricks.*

Knackered

Means absolutely exhausted or very tired

> *No way mate, can't see the end of this movie cause I'm knackered.*

Knickers in a Knot

Means to get upset

> *Okay okay ... no need to get ya knickers in a knot.*

Knock

means to put down or criticise

> *Don't knock it mate, it's the only one we have.*

Knock Back

means to refuse

> *I asked her if she'd go out with me but got a knock back.*

Knock Off

Means to finish working

> *Time to knock off guys, cya tomorrow.*

A Knock-Off

Reference to a counterfeit or replica product

> *I think those golf clubs you bought in Thailand are knock-offs.*

Knocked Up

Means pregnant

Knocker

Reference to somebody who criticises things a lot

> *There's a knocker in every crowd, you just have to get used to it.*

Knockers

Reference to a woman's breasts

Check the knockers out on that chick ... unbelievable!

Knuckle Sandwich

Reference to a punch in the mouth

Be careful or I'll give you a knuckle sandwich.

L

Lair

Means to be a bit flash

That lad's a bit of a lair.

Laid Back

Means to be chilled, easy going, relaxed

This guy's pretty laid back about everything.

Larrikin

Reference to somebody who is a joker or funny person

Laughing Gear

Reference to a person's mouth

Lead Foot

Reference to somebody who speeds a lot

The guy is a lead foot, no wonder he gets speeding tickets.

Leak

Means to urinate

> *I've gotta take a leak, be back soon.*

Left in the Lurch

Means to abandon somebody

> *Looks like she left him in the lurch when she took off.*

Left Out in the Cold

Means to be uninformed, information has not been passed, not included

> *Looks like I've been left out in the cold on this one.*

Leg Opener

Reference to an alcoholic drink, usually spirits

Legend

Reference to somebody who is pretty cool, a great person

> *Thanks for doing that for me mate, you are a legend.*

Lemon

Means faulty product

> *Man I bought myself a lemon when I got this car, it's always breaking down.*

Lippy

Means lipstick

> *Put on some eye shadow and a bit of lippy and wallah ... gorgeous again.*

Liquid Laugh

Reference to vomit

Liquid Lunch

Reference to drinking at lunch time

Lob In

Means to drop in to see someone

> *I'll just lob in when I pass by if that's okay.*

Local Rag

Reference to the local newspaper

Lollies

Means sweets

London to a Brick

Means absolute or certain

> *London to a brick, she'll be back in here within the hour to complain.*

Long in the Tooth

Means old

> *He's a bit long in the tooth to be doing that don't ya think?*

Loo

Reference to toilet

> *I'm off to the loo, back soon.*

Looker

Means a good looking person

> *Wow ... she's a looker.*

Lousy

Means not good, garbage, bad

> *I feel lousy today.*

Lucky Country

Reference to Australia

M

Maccas

Reference to McDonalds restaurants and / or the food sold by McDonalds

> *Might grab some maccas on the way to the drive in ay ... what do ya reckon?*

Mad as a Cut Snake (also Mad as a Meat Axe)

Means crazy, weird

> *My old man's as mad as a cut snake, he'll drink anything.*

Make Do

Means to work with what you've got, cope with

> *I guess we'll just have to make do.*

Map of Tassie

Reference to a female's pubic hair area

> *Yep, she got outa the car and map of tassie for all to see ... she should wear some knickers with a dress like that.*

Mate

Means buddy or friend

Mate's Rates

Means cheaper than usual for a friend

> *Yep got a great deal ... he gave it to me for mate's rates.*

Metho

Means methylated spirits

Middy

Reference to a glass of beer (285ml) in New South Wales

Milk Bar

Reference to a takeaway food shop

Misery Guts

Reference to somebody who is miserable, always complaining

> *Listen to old misery guts, he's go no idea why we're here.*

Missus

Means wife or girlfriend

Mob

Means a group of people

> *Check this mob out, bloody noisy I tell ya.*

Mobs

Means loads of or a lot of

> *I got mobs of em mate, order em when you're ready.*

Molly Coddle

Means to fuss over, wrap in cotton wool

> *No need to molly coddle me on this one, I can look after.*

Mongrel

Usually means a nasty or despicable person

> *The guys who sell this stuff are nothing but mongrels.*

Moo Juice

Means milk

Moolah

Means money

> *Where's all the moolah.*

Mozzie

Reference to a mosquito

Mucking Around

Means acting in a way that others generally don't like

> *These guys are just muckin around at school, time they pulled their socks up I think.*

Muddy

Reference to a mud crab

> *Caught three barra and a muddy, not a bad day's fishing if I say so myself.*

Mug

Means gullible person

> *Check this mug out, he aint gonna go very far at all.*

Can also be a reference to one's face

> *That's one ugly mug I gotta tell ya, only a mother could love it.*

Mullet

Refers to a hairstyle where the back grows long and the rest is cut short

> *Check the mullet out on that guy, looks like crap.*

Munchies

Means to snack or nibble

> *Man I got the munchies tonight ... you got any nuts in the cupboard.*

Mushie

Means mushroom

Muster

Means to round up sheep or cattle

> *The guys have gone to muster the cattle, gonna be days before they get back.*

N

Nasho

An old phrase that meant National Service which is no longer compulsary

> *Those guys who went off to fight in Vietnam were mostly nashos.*

Never Never Land

Reference to the outback or centre of Australia

Nick

Means to steal

> *He nicked that thing.*

Also refers to the condition of something

> *What sort of nick is it in.*

> *Looks like its in good nick.*

Nick Off

Means to go now, get lost

> *Go on ... nick off ... I've had enough of ya bullshit.*

Niggle

Means to dig, have a go at somebody

> *He's been niggling me all day.*

Nipper

Reference to a young surf lifesaver

> *They have a nipper carnival this weekend.*

Also reference to a young child who is not necessarily a junior surf lifesaver

> *Look at those little nippers in the playground ... they're cute at that age.*

Nippy

Means cold temperature

> *Wow, bit nippy today don't you think?*

No Worries (or No Dramas)

Means not a problem, it's okay, don't worry about it, everything is fine (Australian Attitude)

> *No worries mate, I'll take care of it.*
>
> *Yeah ... no dramas, accidents happen.*

No Hoper

Reference to somebody who'll never do well

> *Look at this no hoper, bloody useless if you ask me.*
>
> *If those kids don't go to school they'll just be no hopers.*

Not Worth a Zac

Means something is not worth anything

Nuddy

Means to be naked or nude

> *When we were kids we used to run around in the nuddy everywhere, nobody worried about anything.*

Nuggets

Reference to men's testicles

> *Hang on to ya nuggets mate, this is gonna get rough.*

O

Ocker

Reference to an unsophisticated person

>*He's a bit of an ocker this guy. Funny as too.*

Ocky Strap

Reference to a rubber or elastic strap with hooks on the end

Off The Beaten Track

Means to go off road, leave sealed road, outback

Off Ya Face (or Off My Face)

Means drunk

>*Yep, I was off my face when I got home, can't even remember gettin in bed.*

Offsider

Reference to an assistant or helper or even partner

>*And this is my offsider, couldn't survive without her.*

Oldies

Reference to one's parents

>*I gotta ask the oldies if I can go out tonight mate.*

>*I'm off to the oldies for dinner tonight.*

Old Fart

Reference to an old person

Jack's just an old fart, don't worry about him.

Checkout this old fart, bit of a no hoper if you ask me.

On The Nose

Means to smell

You are on the nose mate.

One Armed Bandit

Reference to a slot machine

Open Their Lunch

Reference to passing of wind or farting

Ok, who opened their lunch? That's disgusting.

Outback

Reference to the central areas of Australia

Ow Ya Goin

Its a question that means how are you

Oz

Reference to Australia

I live in good ole oz mate.

P

Packing It

Means to be scared

> *He was packing it when the old man turned up.*

Pansy

Reference to a soft bloke, someone more effeminate than normal

> *Check the pansy out over there.*

Para

Means paralytic from drinking alcohol

Pash

Means to passionately kiss

> *Yep, pashed her two minutes after I met her ... lucky she'd had a few drinks.*

Past the Black Stump

Means a long way away, the back of nowhere

> *I don't know how far out she lives, somewhere out past the black stump as far as I can tell.*

Pat Malone

Means you are on your own, alone

Yep, I was on my pat malone last night. Was nice and peaceful.

Pav

Referring to pavlova

Pearly Whites

Reference to teeth

Perve

As a verb it means to look at somebody with lust in mind

That's it, why don't you have a good perve mate?

As a noun it is reference to somebody who perves on others

Check this perve out, he can't keep his eyes of her boobs.

Piddle

Means to urinate

I took a piddle around the corner.

Piece of Piss

Means something is easy to do

That's a piece of piss, I'll do it this morning.

Pigs Bum (or Pigs Arse)

Means that's wrong, or incorrect

Pigs bum that's how they do it, they'd get hurt doing that.

Pig's arse you did!

Piker

Reference to a social misfit or a drop out

> *He won't turn up, he usually pikes out.*

> *He didn't come cause he's a piker.*

Piss and Wind

Means something or somebody has no real substance

> *Forget about him, he's all piss and wind.*

Piss In Your Pocket

Means to give lots of praise, almost over praise

> *I don't want to piss in your pocket, but I think you did a great job today.*

Piss Off

Means the same as go away

> *Why don't you piss off mate!*

Piss Up

Means a party with lots of alcohol

Pissed Off

Means angry

Wow, is he pissed off or what?

Pisser

Means very funny

> *That joke was a pisser.*

Play Possum

Means pretending to be asleep

> *He's playing possum with us.*

Play Silly Buggers

Means to be messing around, wasting time

> *These guys are just playing silly buggers, they'll get themselves in trouble for sure.*

Plonk

Reference to cheap wine

> *We can pick up a bottle of plonk on the way to the party.*

Pocket Billiards

Means to play with your testicles through your pockets

Pokies

reference to poker machines found in many licensed premises

> *Might go play the pokies tonight, good way to kill a few hours.*

Pollie

Reference to a politician

> *Which pollie do we vote for today .. I have no idea any more.*

Pom (or Pommie)

Reference to somebody from England / the United Kingdom

Pommie Shower

Means to use deodorant instead of taking an actual shower

> *No time mate, we just took a pommie shower and hit the toe.*

Pong

Means to smell bad

> *That place really ponged.*

Poofter

Reference to a homosexual male

Port

An older term that is reference to a suitcase

> *So he grabbed his port and headed off, never saw him again.*

Postie

Reference to a postman

Pot

Reference to a large beer (usually in Victoria)

> *Can I have three pots thanks mate.*

Pozzy (or Pozzie)

Means position

> *So I took up my pozzy.*

Prang

Means to crash something

> *Sorry mum, I pranged the car on the way home. I promise I'll pay for it.*

Pretty

When connected to a specific phrase it means quite

> *I think she's pretty good looking.*

> *That's a pretty big call you made back there mate.*

Prezzy (or Pressie)

Means present or gift

> *Better buy the kids' pressies now before the christmas rush starts.*

Pull Ya Head In

Means you don't want to listen to somebody and is used to tell them to shut up

Mate, I'm sick of your rambling, time for you to pull your head in I think.

I knew I was in trouble so I pulled my head in pretty quickly.

Pushing Up Daisies

Means dead

Pussy Foot Around

Means trying hard to avoid the issue and not offend

He's pussy footing around, time to say it how it is.

Put The Wind Up

Means to prod, to scare

I had to put the wind up him to get him moving.

Q

Quack

Reference to a doctor

Off to the quacks are you?

Queer

Reference to a homosexual male

Make a Quid

Means to earn a living

I don't mind this job, it's helping me make a quid before I retire.

Not the Full Quid

Reference to somebody of low intelligence

Something's wrong with him alright .. he aint the full quid!

R

Rack Off

Means to get lost or get out of here, to tell somebody to leave, they're not wanted here

Time for you to rack off mate, you've over stayed your welcome.

Time for me to rack off guys, cya tomorrow.

Rage

Means a trend

You gotta get one of these, they're all the rage.

Rage On

Means to continue partying

Man they raged on till about 4 this morning.

Rapt

Means pleased, delighted

She was rapt when I gave her the iPad.

Rare as Rockin Horse Shit

Means very scarce

> *Tried to buy a second hand TP fairway wood, but they're rare as rockin horse shit. Probably cost me an arm and a leg if I can find one.*

Rat Bag

Is a mild insult when not used with a friend.

> *That guy is nothing but a rat bag.*

It can also be a friendly term used to stir in a friendly way

> *Hey ya rat bag.*

Raw Prawn

Means to be generally disagreeable

> *Don't come the raw prawn with me mate.*

Reckon

Means opinion or thoughts that one might have

> *What do you reckon mate?*

> *Yep, that's what I reckon.*

Can also mean for sure

> *Yep ... I reckon!*

Reffo

Reference to a refugee

A boatload of reffos turn up and suddenly there's a shit load of navy people in town.

Reg Grundies

Reference to undies or underwear

Bag busted open on the carousel and there were reg grundies everywhere.

Rego

Reference to vehicle registration

Gotta pay the rego bill this month.

Rellie

Reference to a family relative

Goin to the rellies for the weekend, should be fun.

Ridgie Didge

True or genuine article, an original

Worth takin a look at ... if it's ridgie didge it'll be worth a packet in a few years time.

Ring In

Reference to a substitute

The captain got injured so they brought in a ring in.

Ripper

Means great, awesome, very good

> *She tells a ripper yarn after a few drinks ... you gotta invite her to the barbie.*

Rip Off

Reference to a bad deal or something that is over priced

> *Fifty bucks! What a rip off.*

Road Train

Reference to a big semi trailer with multiple trailers

Rock Up

Means to turn up, arrive

> *What time are you gonna rock up mate?*

Rollie

Reference to a cigarette that you roll yourself

> *The second tyre went flat so we pulled over to the side and lit up a rollie ... no point worrying about it.*

Root

Means to have sex

> *So ... did you get a root?*

Rooted

Means very tired

> *Had a huge weekend, was rooted by Sunday night.*

Can also means ruined or broken

> *Don't buy that boat mate, the engine's rooted.*

Rope-able

Means extremely angry

> *I forgot to get the concert tickets in time, she was rope-able when she found out.*

Rort

Means to cheat or defraud, can also mean something is over-privileged

> *What a rort that is ... politicians getting upgraded to first class for free!*

Rotten

Means to be drunk

> *I drank way too much last night, was rotten before ten.*

Rubbish Someone

Means to criticize a person

> *He's shouldn't be rubbishing him like that, he's trying his best.*

Rug Up

Means to put on warm clothes, jackets etc

Time to rug up mate, it's getting pretty cool.

S

Salty

Reference to a salt water crocodile

Salvos

Reference to the Salvation Army and also its members

Yeah he's a salvo, been doin it for years.

Sanger (or Sanga)

Reference to a sandwich

They had free beer and wine and chucked out a few sangers for everybody to chew on.

Schooner

Reference to a large glass of beer in Queensland and New South Wales

Scorcher

Means very hot

It's going to be a scorcher today.

Scratchie

Reference to an instant lottery ticket where you scratch the panels on the front of it to reveal prizes

Might pick up a scratchie and a newspaper while I'm in town.

Servo

Reference to a petrol station which used to be called a service state

Pull in to the next servo, we'll fill er up there.

Session

To go out drinking

Cya babe, goin down to the pub for a session with the boys.

Shag

Means sexual intercourse

Shaggin Wagon

Reference to a panel van

Shank's Pony

Means to travel on foot

How will I get there ... by shank's pony of course ... I aint made of money.

Shark Biscuit

Reference to a new surfer

Checkout the shark biscuit on his new boogie board.

She's Apples

It's alright, everything is okay; giving someone assurance

> *Don't worry about it mate, she's apples.*

She'll Be Right

Means it will be okay

> *Hey, she'll be right mate, just let the smoke settle down before you go home.*

Sheila

Reference to a girl or a woman

> *She's one great sheila that one.*

> *I was standing there minding me own business and suddenly this sheila comes up to me.*

Shellacking

Means to be defeated by a huge margin

> *We got a shellacking today, they were just too good.*

Shit Faced

Means to be very drunk

> *Had a great night last night, got shit faced ... no idea how I got back home.*

Shit Load

Means a lot

> *I don't know exactly how many but it was a shit load!*

Shonky

Means dubious, underhanded

> *Where did I get it? Don't ask ... was a bit of a shonky deal.*

Shoot Through

Means to leave

> *Listen, I gotta shoot through, time to start my night shift.*

Shout

A term used in a bar or pub and means to buy a round of drinks

> *It's your shout mate.*

Show You The Ropes

Means to guide you, to show you how to do something or where to go

> *Come with me, I'll show you the ropes.*

Shut Ya Gob

Means to be quiet, an aggressive statement.

> *Hey ... shut ya gob ... I won't cop anybody talking about my girl like that!*

Sickie

Means to have a day off due to illness

> *Karen isn't here, she took a sickie.*

Skimpy

Means barely clothed, not much covering flesh

> *Did you see the skimpy bikinis those chicks were wearin at the beach ... no wonder there's a million guys hanging around.*

Skint

Means to be broke

> *I'm skint mate, can you take care of it?*

Skite

To boast or brag about something

> *Yeah we saw it ... no need to skite about it mate.*

Slab

Reference to a carton of beer

> *Let's pick up a slab on the way to Steve's.*

Slash

Means to urinate (for a man)

Sleep Out

Reference to a house verandah converted to a bedroom

We made a sleep out for the kids, so much more space now.

Smoko

Means a smoke or coffee break

Time for smoko boys, the pie van's here.

Snag

Reference to a sausage

Snags and onions on a bun ... best brekkie you've ever eaten if you've been in the bush for a few days.

Snog

Means to kiss

Check those two out snogging over there.

Snot

Means to hit

He wouldn't let up so I snotted him.

Snot Rag

Reference to a handkerchief

Sook

Reference to somebody who is soft or easily offended or upset

Man that guy's a sook ... one bad comment and he's off tellin his mum.

Souped Up

Means the engine of a car has been hotted up for more power

> *You oughta see the ute steve drives, it's all souped up and got a set of wheels that'll blow ya mind.*

Sparrow's Fart

Means very early, at dawn

> *It's an early flight in the morning, gotta get up at sparrow's fart to catch it.*

Spew

Means to vomit

Spewin

Means very angry

> *I told the oldies about the car scratch yesterday, the old man was spewin.*

Spit the Dummy

Means to get very upset at something

> *Hey mate, no need to spit the dummy, that aint gonna fix it.*

Spot On

Means exactly right

> *He was spot on when he told us who would win today.*

Sprung

Means to be caught doing something

> *Yep, me and the missus was havin some fun and got sprung by the kids.*

Spunk

Reference to a good looking person

> *When he came into the club we couldn't take our eyes off him, what a spunk!*

Squiz

Means to take a look at something

> *Come on ... let's take a squiz before we go.*

Station

Means a big farm or grazing property

> *He owns a station in northern territory somewhere.*

Sticky Beak

Reference to a nosy person

> *The neighbours are sticky beaks, they should mind their own business.*

Stoked

Means very pleased

> *I bought her some flowers and she was stoked.*

Strewth

An exclamation

> *Strewth! Did you see how fast he was going?*

Strides

Means trousers

Stroppy

Means to be angry or cranky

> *Why's he so stroppy tonight?*

Stubby

Reference to a 375ml bottle of beer

Stubby Holder

A beer bottle cooler made of neoprene in most cases today

Stuffed

Means tired

> *Can't go tonight mate, I'm stuffed.*

Can also be an expression of surprise.

Well I'll be stuffed, checkout the size of that thing.

Pull Up Stumps

Means to move home

Stunned Mullet

Means to be surprised, bewildered, uncomprehending

> *I told her what the kid did and she looked at me like a stunned mullet.*

> *He stood there like a stunned mullet when they read out the results.*

Sucked In

Means tricked, deceived

> *We all got sucked in by his story.*

Sun Bake

Means to sunbathe

Sunnies

Reference to sunglasses

Surfie

A person who goes surfing and normally more than they go to work!

Swag

Reference to a roll up canvas bed for camping

> *Stuff the hotel, I'd rather camp in my swag tonight.*

Can also means a large number of things

> *We went out to the bush and there were swags of flies, got covered in em.*

Swagman

A term used to refer to a tramp or hobo

T

Ta

Means thanks or thank you

Tall Poppies

Reference to people perceived as being very successful

Tall Poppy Syndrome

This is the tendency to criticize successful people and knock them down off their platform

Tart Yourself Up

Means to dress up in your best clothes

Technicolor Yawn

Means to vomit

Tee-Up

Means to set up something

> *Let's tee up a suitable time to catch up.*

Thongs

Slip on flats with two straps across the top of the foot, sometimes called flip flops

Throw a Wobbly (or Chuck a Wobbly)

Means to go mad

> *Can you believe it, I got in 5 minutes late and he still chucked a wobbly.*

Tickets On Yourself

Means to have a high opinion of oneself

> *She's got a few tickets on herself if you ask me.*

Tight Arse

Means to be mean with money

> *Don't ask him for anything, he's too much of a tight arse to give anything away.*

Tinny

A can of beer or a small aluminium boat

Toey

Means to be touchy, sensitive or nervous

> *He looks a bit toey.*

Togs

Reference to swimming costume, bathers, budgies

Too Right

Means definitely

> *Q. Hey mate, ya wanna open a tinny?*
>
> *A. Too right mate.*

Top End

Reference to the far north of Australia

Trackies (also Trackie Dacks)

Means track suit

> *Just wearin my trackies mate.*

Tramp Stamps

A reference to tattoos on a woman or girl

Trots (also Runs)

Means diarrhea

> *I got a case of the trots.*

Truckie

A truck driver

True Blue

Means very patriotic

> *That sheila is a true blue aussie.*

Tucker

Means food

Tucker Bag

Means food bag

Tuff Stickers

This is a reference to tattoos as worn by a male.

> *Checkout the bloke with the tuff stickers.*

Turn It Up

Means stop what your saying or doing as its not right

> *Come on mate, turn it up. I think he's had enough.*

Turps

Usually mean turpentine though it can also mean alcohol.

> *Let's hit the turps buddy, time for a binge.*

Two Up

This is a gambling game played by spinning two coins simultaneously and looking for combinations of head and tails

Two Pot Screamer

Somebody who gets drunk very easily

> *The missus is a two pot screamer, can't get her off the dance floor once she starts.*

Two Shakes of a Duck's Tail

Means a short time

> *I'll be there in two shakes of a duck's tail.*

U

Unco

Means uncoordinated

Undies

Reference to underwear

Uni

Means university

Up Yaself

Means to have a high opinion of yourself

You're a bit up yaself I think.

Useless as an Ashtray on a Motorbike

Means totally incompetent, useless or unhelpful

Useless as Tits on a Bull

[As above]

Ute

Reference to a utility vehicle with an open back

V

Veggies

Means vegetables

Vee Dub

Reference to a volkswagen beetle

Veg Out

Means to relax, usually in front of the TV

> *Gonna kick back and veg out tonight mate, drop by if you want.*

Veggo

Reference to a vegetarian

> *He's veggo mate, you better chuck some spinach on ya list.*

Verbal Diarrhea

Means to talk shit

W

Waffle

Means to talk a lot of nonsense

> *He's always waffling on.*

Wagging School

Means to be truant or absent from school without permission

A Walkover

Reference to somebody who is easy to defeat

> *He'll be a walkover for you.*

Wanker

Reference to a person who is an idiot

> *This guy's a wanker, don't believe a word he says.*

Wanna

Means do you want to

> *Hey mate, wanna go get a beer?*

Wedding Tackle

Reference to a man's genitals

Whinge

Means to complain

Whipper Snipper

Reference to a nylon cord grass trimmer

White Pointers

Reference to the breasts of a topless female sunbather

White Ant

Means to undermine or to criticise what somebody else says or does

The last thing we want is somebody white anting us.

Wombat

Reference to a person who eats, roots and leaves

Woos (or Wuss)

Means coward or chicken

What a wuss this guy is.

Wouldn't Be Dead For Quids

Means having a great time, great to be alive

Wowser

A spoilsport

> *He won't turn up, he's a wowser.*

X

XXXX

Four X (or Fourex) is a brand of Queensland beer

Y

Yabber

Means to talk a lot

> *Man oh man this guy can yabber.*

Yakka

Reference to work

> *It's hard yakka putting these Ikea shelves together.*

Yarn

Means story

> *He tells a great yarn.*

Yewy

Means a U-turn in traffic

> *Time to chuck a yewy mate, hang on.*

Yobbo

Reference to an ignorant person

What a yobbo he is, time to move tables.

Yonks

Means a long time period

It's been yonks since we went to town.

Youse

Means you people (plural)

Hey what are youse doin for dinner tonight?

Z

Zack

Means cheap, also a reference to a sixpence (old equivalent of the current 5 cents)

Won't cost you a zack mate ... he's givin em away.

Zonked

Means to be very tired

I am absolutely zonked.

That's It Mate

Holy mackerel, I'm done. Come visit us down-under soon.

Cya

About The Author - George Lee Sye

George Lee Sye's fascination with human behaviour started in the mid 1980s. Intent on understanding how to accelerate the process of building connection and rapport with people in his work, he began a journey of discovery that has now influenced every aspect of his life, both personal and professional.

Through his seminars, personal coaching, audio and printed books, George has devoted himself to passing on his knowledge and skill for creating a remarkable quality of life. What he has learnt through reading, trial and error and an incredible diversity of experiences is now the foundation for positively impacting the lives of literally thousands of people.

George's style of writing is somewhat unusual. As he says, he writes like he talks. His goal has always been to communicate to people in simple and practical terms using life examples that people can relate to. His success in this area has come predominantly through his belief that delivering an idea without a way of using it is nothing more than giving people another topic of conversation. Unless the idea converts to some form of action or behavioural change that positively affects a person's life, it is a waste of time.

His ability to simplify what are often considered to be complex topics is remarkable. As a result, he has been able to create considerable value for companies with whom he has worked in the area of business improvement, and his popularity as a corporate educator, speaker and personal coach has grown consistently.

For more information about George and his work, you should visit his personal website at www.georgeleesye.com or his training platform at www.9skillsfactory.com

---------- END ----------

Printed in Great Britain
by Amazon